Problems

RESOURCES FOR BIBLICAL LIVING

Problems

Solving Them God's Way

JAY ADAMS

P&R

P U B L I S H I N G
P.O. BOX 817 • PHILLIPSBURG • NEW JERSEY 08865-0817

Printed in the United States of America

ISBN: 978-1-59638-184-1

"I'VE GOT A PROBLEM." How often have you heard those words on the lips of your friends? Or, for that matter, on your own? Problems usually mean trouble. And there's no doubt about it, trouble abounds. Indeed, a man who was quite familiar with problems once exclaimed, "Man who is born of a woman is few of days and full of trouble" (Job 14:1). Life is short, Job observed, and what there is of it is full of difficulty! Yes, that's the way it is and has been, ever since Adam and Eve wrongly handled the problem of an intruder in the garden. There were no problems until the serpent raised a question—the first question in history—about God's Word and his intentions. Then our first parents were faced with the world's first problem: "What should we believe about and how should we act on this new thought that has been introduced into our minds? Should we obey our Creator, who forbade us to eat of the tree of the knowledge of good and evil? Or should we . . . ?" You know the rest. As the result of their foolish solution, we now have problems with ourselves, with other people, with God, with ideas, with things—you name it. Life was not intended to be so full of problems, but ever since Eden, it has become virtually problem-oriented. Problems! Problems! Problems! Always problems!

Problem-Solving as Part of Life

Since the fall of Adam, life has been truly described as a succession of problems. A central problem of living that one must solve is how to turn problem-oriented living into solution-oriented living—how to experience a life of successive solutions. Is such a thing possible? In particular, Christian, because you live in a world that is filled with problems, many of which are arrayed against your faith, do you sometimes wonder whether it is possible for you to find solutions that will enable you successfully to experience a victorious life? The world keeps churning up one problem after another, so that after a while you may be tempted to throw in the towel and give up. Well, surprising as it may seem to you, Christian, of all people, *you are the one who can become a superb problem-solver.*

Problem-Solving as a Christian

How is that? Why is it possible for the Christian to be the world's problem-solver, *par excellence*? That's what I will explain in this booklet: how you, as a believer, have an advantage over everyone else when it comes to solving problems.

To begin with, it's important for you to recognize that you cannot avoid problem-solving. Nor should you. For instance, when unavoidable problems arise because of your faith, you must accept the challenge of solving them. Suffering, perhaps, is the greatest of these problems. Peter writes, "If when you do good and suffer for it you endure, this is a gracious thing in the sight of God" (1 Peter 2:20). The Roman government offered believers a solution to the problem of persecution: to call Caesar "Lord," and sacrifice to the emperor as God. It was quick, easy, and possible for every believer to accept this solution. But if one loved Jesus, such a solution was totally unacceptable. It meant denying his lordship. And it meant worshiping a false god. Christians, who would do neither, went by the thousands to their deaths because they refused the solution offered to them. Instead, their solution—God's solution—was to face willingly lions and gladiators in the Colosseum. The solution was hard, but uncomplicated. And like the solution in the garden, this solution involved making a choice—a choice for or against God. Indeed, one of the facts to learn is that *all* choices are in essence the same—all solutions are either for or against God. Yet not all solutions are as straightforward as this.

There are many other problems that you must solve: how to make a living, what kind of car to buy, what to eat tonight, what clothes to wear today, whether to see the doctor or tough it out, and so forth. Usually, these are not pressing problems that entail such significant consequences as "Will you or will you not sacrifice to Caesar?" In other words, these decisions, while constituting a major portion of those problems that we must solve every day, ordinarily do not have life-changing outcomes. Yet they must be made. In fact, unless a person learns to make the myriad of small decisions cheerfully that he must address every day of his life, he may become annoyed by them, thus adding to the misery of existence that such easily irritated persons already experience.

Christians, however, have every reason to be happy people who are well adjusted to ordinary life problems, which they do not find to be irksome, but rather a joy to be able to face in a world that God has made and enables them to enjoy. They are thankful for food, automobiles, and the clothing that they have to wear. Thus, solving life's ordinary problems, as a whole, is not a chore but a pleasure. I mention this because there are people who become exhausted over making the many choices that such problem-solving entails. They are usually the ones who lament, "Life is nothing more than problems, problems, problems!" No Christian ought to be found among that crowd. Instead, Christians ought to be known for their happy acceptance of God's providential work in their lives. They recognize that day by day God sends them good and perfect gifts from above, which work together for their good (Rom. 8:28–29).

Do you live a life of gratitude for every problem you're privileged to solve? If not, think of them this way: "Every time I'm called on to solve a problem, making the decisions involved in doing so provides me with one more opportunity to please

7

God by making choices that honor him. That's one way to demonstrate my love for him."

Problems You Cannot Solve

On the other hand, there are problems that you will *never* solve because the solution to them doesn't lie within your power. When Paul was imprisoned at Rome, he heard about envious brothers who were preaching out of rivalry, "thinking," as he said, "to afflict me in my imprisonment" (Phil. 1:17). That was a terrible thing for them to do. Now, Paul might have seen only that side of the problem. But he didn't. What was his response to these misguided brothers? He wrote, "What then? Only that in every way, . . . Christ is proclaimed, and in that I rejoice" (1:18). He could do nothing to alter the situation, and so he found in it—bad as it was—something for which he could give thanks to God. Sometimes that is *all* you can do, but when you do so, the problem takes on a new complexion. Its "solution" (so far as your attitude is concerned) is to recognize the providential working of God and bow before it.

Then there are solutions that, if he so desires, only God can provide. We have no business attempting to solve problems that fall into this category. There are matters that God has kept secret, as well as those that he has revealed to us (Deut. 29:29). We have no right to pry into the former; they belong to God alone. To do so is nothing short of attempted theft. For instance, God hasn't told us what our dead loved ones are now doing—or, as we sometimes put it, why they die "before their time." He hasn't revealed the time of Christ's return, though from time to time there are those who cause a stir in the church by predicting it. God has kept such information to himself. It is a part of those "secret things" about which we ought not to inquire, since he hasn't revealed them to us. To frequent spiritualists, play around with Ouija boards, or probe into theories about aspects of the afterlife concerning which God has not spoken is to defy him. To engage in such defiance is to question his providential dealings with us. It implies that we think we're wiser than he. On the other hand, to fail to understand and appropriate what he *has* revealed is an act of negligence.

There are Christians who fail on either one side or the other of this matter, and some on both sides of it. The inquisitive aspect of our nature will find more than adequate satisfaction in the proper study of what God *has* revealed; there is no need to pry into things that do not belong to us. The problem with most of those who attempt to enter into the things that God has kept to himself is that they spend far too little time learning what he has already revealed! Many find their faith inadequate because they know so little about it. These are people who may read their Bibles from time to time, but have never spent time truly studying the Scriptures. They spend far more time in front of a television than they do learning about their Lord, and they know far more about sports and entertainment than they do about him! With such little knowledge, it is understandable why such people often make bad decisions in addressing problem situations.

The Problem of Avoiding Problem-Solving

Some people make every effort to avoid solving problems. They attempt to palm off the decisions that they must make onto other people. Actually, it is impossible to live that way. Were you to make the ultimate decision to avoid *all* problems, you might find yourself confined to a mental hospital. There, others decide what you will do. Many problems are "solved" for you. But even then, when one attempts to turn over his responsibility for solving problems to others, he still isn't able to avoid them. Those "others" will restrict him, overmedicate him, destroy his brain cells through shock therapy, or inflict dozens of other insults

9

on his body that cause him all sorts of trouble. By attempting to give up his responsibility to solve problems, not only does he fail to achieve his goal, he sets himself up for innumerable problems. He may even have to face the problem of extricating himself from such an environment.

Troublesome problems are everywhere. Like a wireless Internet signal, they follow you wherever you go. There is no escaping them. So you must learn how to solve them.

Problems You Must Solve

The problems you face are of two kinds: (1) those that you bring upon yourself, and (2) those that are thrust upon you. Since you still sin, even though you have been given a new life that enables you to overcome sin, many of your problems are of your own making. You find yourself saying such things as, "Why did I say that to my wife?" or "There I go, lying again," or "Do I really believe what I claim to believe?" or "How am I going to clean up the mess I made?"

Indeed, if you are honest about it, you must admit that you yourself are a problem! Why is this so? You were born a sinner, and as such, you learned many sinful ways of thinking, speaking, and acting. Then you were saved. But that didn't automatically erase all the patterns of living that you had developed. Because remnants of the old life remain within you as habit patterns, which you have not yet overcome by replacing them with their biblical alternatives, you continue to sin. Truly, therefore, much of the trouble that you experience is self-inflicted. By your sinful actions, words, and thoughts, you manufacture new problems for yourself day by day. Surely, if you engage in any amount of reflection on your life, you will agree with this assessment of things.

So instead of creating more problems for yourself and others, you must learn how to live according to God's new ways.

These godly ways, rather than multiplying such problems, provide solutions to them.

But then there are problems for which you are not responsible that may give you a great amount of difficulty. As I said above, they are thrust upon you. Interestingly, our English word *problem* comes from a Greek term, *problema*, which refers to something "pushed or thrust forward"—something that may jut out before someone as an obstacle. While you can avoid many problems by learning to walk according to God's ways so as not to bring problems on yourself, other problems come to you, uninvited, which it is impossible to avoid. So you must deal with them.

You must learn how to solve both sorts of problems: those that are of your own making and those that are not. What we want to discover is *how* you can do so.

Is This My Problem?

But before tackling that matter in depth, let me stress the fact that it isn't necessary to solve all the problems of which you become aware. In Proverbs 27:12, the writer says, "The prudent sees danger and hides himself, but the simple go on and suffer for it." In other words, it's foolish to walk into trouble when you can walk around it. Often, people who want to prove themselves capable get involved in problems that they have no need to face. Others seem to seek out trouble when they ought to stay clear of it. For instance, Proverbs 26:17 sets forth this principle in graphic terms: "Whoever meddles in a quarrel is like one who takes a passing dog by the ears." If a problem isn't your concern, then why get bitten by it?

Then there are problems that you may choose whether to solve or not. In the Corinthian church, brothers were doing things to one another that would have constituted cause for bringing lawsuits (1 Cor. 6:1–5). Paul forbade going to law before unbelievers, but said that these brothers could adjudicate such matters on their own as a Christian church. Of interest to our concerns, however, he *also* indicated that if a believer chose to do so, he might simply take it on the chin: "Why not rather suffer wrong? Why not rather be defrauded?" (6:7). Sometimes, then, you must solve problems in ways that are permissible, but not necessarily expedient. When reflecting on another problem elsewhere, Paul wrote, "All things are lawful for me, but all things are not expedient" (6:12; 10:23 KJV).

So in order to reach good solutions to such problems, you must first learn how to distinguish between those things that are lawful but not expedient, and those problems that God requires you to solve.[1] And you must remember that to try to solve the latter by not solving them *is* to solve them—the wrong way.

Moreover, some problems will never be satisfactorily solved in your lifetime by you or by anyone else. Some problems, like those of "the poor [whom] you will always have with you" (Matt. 26:11 NIV), as Jesus observed, are beyond solving in this era. It will take the coming of the new heaven and the new earth to solve that problem. Problems in understanding the purposes of God's providential working may never be solved in this life: "Why, when I've worked so hard, did Fred, who puts far less into his work than I, receive that promotion and I didn't?" It's usually wrong to struggle with such issues or go beyond recognizing the obvious answer that God willed them, and that he does all things well. To do so is to manufacture problems unnecessarily. Moreover, much of the questioning that God's children engage in isn't really about problem-solving at all; it's nothing but covert rebellion. Those questions that begin with the word *Why*, therefore, ought to be examined carefully to be sure that they are not a veiled form of protest against God's sovereign providence.

1. For information about biblical discernment, see my book *A Call to Discernment* (Eugene, OR: Harvest House, 1987; repr., Stanley, NC: Timeless Texts, 1999).

It is important to know when to attempt to solve problems that you should solve, and when not to solve problems that you shouldn't. You must realize that there are problems that you may solve only at a later time, when more data are acquired, when you have grown spiritually mature enough to solve them, or when you get the new perspective that distance provides you. A seminary student doesn't need to have the solutions to all the problems that a minister of the gospel does. It isn't possible for a businessman to know all there is to know about the work that his employees do. The solutions to many problems that face a company must be made at the lower levels of the organization. On the other hand, some people at those levels think they can solve problems that they really don't understand from their place in the hierarchy. They are quick to offer simple solutions that, if they ever attain to the level of management, they will recognize they were not yet equipped to solve.

As with quick decisions, easy solutions are frequently the wrong ones. Good solutions are reached mostly through taking time, giving thought, putting forth effort, and using the wisdom that comes from experience.

Which Problems Are Mine to Solve?

Since you can't avoid all problems, the only satisfactory answer to *that* problem is to learn how to solve those you can. Then leave the others alone! A sign on the wall of one Christian counselor's office read, "Problems are for solving." That reminder is one that you would do well to put in a prominent place in your home. It was intended to indicate that God has a solution to *every problem that hinders you from living righteously.* Not necessarily to every problem that you encounter, but to those that would otherwise prohibit you from doing God's will. In 2 Peter 1:3 we read that God "has granted to us all things that pertain to life and godliness." This means that not only can we discover how to have eternal life from studying the Scriptures, but we can also know how to solve every problem that arises as we seek to live a godly Christian life. Sometimes learning to live with a problem (as Paul did after unsuccessfully praying for relief from the thorn in his flesh) is the proper response to it.

The sign on the wall further implies not only that you may find those solutions that you need, but that by appropriating them *you'll be able to actually solve those problems*. The Scriptures are practical, not merely theoretical. They point not only to the *what-to*'s but also to the *how-to*'s of Christian living. It's one thing to have a solution that's feasible and another to have one that isn't. God never calls on you to do that which isn't feasible, given the resources that he has provided for you. First Corinthians 10:13 is explicit about this. That verse contains three promises:

1. God will not send a trial your way that others haven't also experienced and met successfully.
2. God will not send any trial your way that is beyond your present ability to handle successfully (if, of course, you handle it his way).
3. God will not so prolong the trial that there is no way out of it; you can look forward to its cessation.

These three promises are based on his faithfulness. If any of them were to fail, you would have the right to conclude that God is not faithful to his promises—that he cannot be depended on to keep his Word—which, of course, is absurd. This verse should be a great comfort and encouragement, especially with regard to solving problems. In effect, one may conclude from it that God sends his children no problems they *should* solve that they *can't* solve, as long as they solve them according to his divinely revealed principles.

In addition to the two facts mentioned above, you may rightly infer a third principle from the placard in the counseling room. It is that *solutions pleasing to God* are both available and applicable. God has made all sorts of solutions to life's problems readily obtainable for you. In his Word he has set them forth by both precept and example. The world is ever offering its own solutions. Scientists, politicians, pundits, family, friends, and a host of others will provide you with a wide array of solutions. But when you examine them carefully, you'll discover that many (probably most) of them are out of accord with God's expressed will. The standard by which all solutions must be judged as to their acceptability to God is his written Word, in which his declarative will[2] is set forth.

The Believer as a Problem-Solver

Perhaps you're thinking, "Well, maybe a biblical counselor can discover and employ God-pleasing ways to handle problems, but I'm just a Christian layman. How can *I* be expected to do so?" The question is appropriate, since so many people today depend on others—especially "experts"—to assume their responsibilities for them. But any biblical counselor worth his salt won't just guide his counselees, helping them to solve problems; he'll also teach counselees how they may solve problems God's way. He considers that task an essential part of the counsel he offers.[3] The last thing he wishes is to have a counselee become dependent on him. As the old saying goes, his goal is not to give him a fish; it's to teach him how to fish. In that regard, it's altogether possible that you will not need to see a counselor if you closely follow the principles set forth in this booklet. They are written by a Christian counselor, it's true, but they are based

2. God's declarative will is that which he has declared in the Scripture as his will to obey. His decretive will is that by which he has determined all things that come to pass.

3. See my book *Teaching to Observe* (Stanley, NC: Timeless Texts, 1996) for further help concerning this matter.

on the Bible—a book that God gave to *every* Christian to solve life's problems. God is a problem-solver, and he wants you to become one, too.

God as a Problem-Solver

True problem-solving began when God solved man's principal problem: how guilty sinners could be forgiven by a holy God. The answer he gave was to send Jesus Christ, his own Son, to die on the cross in the place of sinners who, if they trust in him as Savior, not only will be forgiven but, instead of the punishment they deserve, will obtain eternal life. This was the grand solution of all solutions. In it are embedded the solutions to all other problems as well. If a just God could provide a way to forgive people without thereby violating his justice, surely he can provide solutions to all lesser problems. But please note that it cost him to do so.

The problem is that men have decided that they have better solutions than God's. Early on in the world's history, sinners determined that they'd give up on God and go about solving the sin-spawned problems that they faced. They made objects of wood, stone, and metal that they could manipulate as they pleased. Yet they soon became enamored of them and began to believe their own lies. Things grew from bad to worse so that, soon, faithless Jews were sacrificing their children to appease false gods. Coupled with these foolish ways, the worship of sun, moon, stars, and even animals became prevalent. And when men determined to worship animals, they began to live like them. Someone has said that no one rises higher than the god he worships. Where people worship cows, you can see this idea at work in their standard of living.

So because men who knew truth suppressed it in unrighteousness and turned to these false gods, God gave them up.

The terrible words "God gave them up . . ." that occur twi̇
Romans 1 (vv. 24, 26) all too vividly express the situation: h
gave them up to do those things that were consistent with their
apostasy from the true God. The sordid picture painted in the
words of Romans 1:18–32 describes how very wrong men have
been when allowed to go their own way, attempting to solve the
problems of life as they thought best.

As a Christian, you must ever steer clear of sinful human
solutions. Why would you turn to them when God's good solutions are available to you?

Where to Find Solutions to Problems

All such solutions are found in God's Word. The Bible isn't
a book full of problems, as some consider it to be; rather, it's a
book full of solutions. Given that fact, how does one go about
appropriating them? It isn't enough to believe that God has
provided solutions to problems of life and godliness; you must
learn how to avail yourself of them. I have set forth a simple,
explicit plan for finding and using those solutions. It consists
of two elements:

1. Learning how to find biblical principles that will enable
   you to reach solutions to problems that you are responsible to solve.
2. Learning how to make use of the biblical solutions that
   you find to solve solvable problems.

While it is not possible to provide an entire course in Bible
interpretation and usage[4] in this limited space, nevertheless,
this booklet will teach you the basic principles you will need to
become a biblical problem-solver. They are as follows:

4. You may find such a course of study in my book *What to Do on Thursday* (Stanley,
NC: Timeless Texts, 1995).

problem in biblical language (avoid contem-
)n).

)cation of those passages of Scripture that
)ur problem so that you are able to find them
n needed.

3. Take time to interpret carefully the meaning and purposes for which each of these passages was given[5] (using
substantive helps such as Bible dictionaries and commentaries[6]).

4. Discover the general or specific principles learned from
this study of Scripture and how each of these applies to
your problem.

5. Before the problem occurs or recurs, consider how each
passage generally directs you to think or act when faced
with the problem to which it refers.

6. Ahead of time, determine how the principles in the passage may be applied in concrete ways to each problem
that you encounter.

7. Resolve to do whatever it is you learned from your study
that God wants you to do about the problem.

8. Ask God to help you carry out your resolve. Then *do* it.

How does this eight-point procedure look in a specific case?
Consider the following:

Some Examples

John knows that he has difficulty with lustful thoughts.
He has struggled to overcome the problem. But he's discov-
ered that the desire and the struggle to change fail to achieve
his goal. So he begins to follow the process just outlined.

---

5. Always use passages for the purposes for which they were given. In that way their
full power will be unleashed.

6. Problem-solving requires work. The Bible must be *studied*, not merely read.

He's aware that he finds the strongest temptation in two main places: at work, involving several women who work near him; and at church, where he must mingle closely with other women. He defines his problem as the inability to keep his eyes, and resultant thoughts, from these women. He must learn, therefore, how passages such as Job 31:1, Matthew 5:27–30, and 2 Peter 2:14 apply to his situation. Job's covenant with his eyes involved not looking. John will have to devise ways of diverting his attention as well. He will develop specific actions to take whenever the temptation comes. He will also recognize that to turn his eyes away means turning his thinking away as well.

John will then memorize the chosen verses—or at least their location—for future use in warning himself against, avoiding, or extricating himself from the problem. He'll especially need to come to an understanding of the concept of radical amputation that Jesus set forth in the Matthew 5 passage. Now, having done so, he'll think positively about Job's solution, among others found in Scripture, for avoiding or not giving in to this problem. He'll recall how, when tempted by the evil one, Jesus responded each time with appropriate Scripture that countered the tempter's suggestion. John will learn to do the same. All along, he'll use 2 Peter 2:14 as an impetus to take concrete action. As he peruses that verse's context, he'll find much to loathe about the lifestyle he seeks to avoid. Becoming disgusted with himself as he reads, he should find his desire to overcome the temptation increasing. Throughout, however, his *prime* motivation will be to please God.

Mary has a wagging tongue. She comes to recognize her proclivity to receive and disseminate gossip. Using her concordance, she will locate some principal passages on the subject (for instance, Prov. 10:18; 11:13; 18:8; 20:19; 26:20–22). As John did, she will familiarize herself with the locations, meanings, and purposes of each of these passages. She'll recognize the sad effects of gossip mentioned in them (causing contention, separating friends, and the like), and, of greatest importance, the displeasure that the Lord has with gossips. So as part of her motivation, she will determine to refrain from the temptation to gossip or to receive it from others. She will also plan to stop consuming gossip like candy, and by going on a "conversation diet" from which gossip is eliminated as harmful, she will refuse to dine on it any longer—even when attractively served by others. Should she unthinkingly take a bite, she will immediately spit it out before consuming the entire piece. In addition, recognizing that the tongue can set the world on fire (James 3:1–12), Mary will refuse to add fuel to any brush fires she encounters so as to keep them from spreading. Finally, she will explain to others that she is determined to refrain from the use of gossip, thus putting herself out on a limb, and reducing the amount of gossip that others will provide for her consumption. Throughout it all, once again, the focus must be on pleasing God.

In each case, specific, concrete plans, which are laid out beforehand and promptly executed whenever problems are encountered, will be the key to the problem-solver's solution. These plans should include both ways of amputating (putting off the undesirable sinful response to a problem) and positive ways of putting on new, alternative, God-pleasing ways to deal with it.

God's Promise of Help

In all of this, it's essential to remember that God promises you the help you will need. He doesn't leave you to your own ingenuity or your own efforts to solve your problems. Paul says, "It is God who works in you, both to will and to work for his good pleasure" (Phil. 2:13). Never forget that encouraging promise! You're not in this alone. If you ask God, he'll enable you to do the things that have been mentioned above, thus leading to the proper solutions to problems that might otherwise cause much grief. God makes you both willing *and* desirous to solve problems his way. And he provides the power to do so. What more could you ask for?

So it's not by your wisdom, your ingenuity, your power, or your goodness that you'll be able to solve problems God's way. When the disciples couldn't cast out a demon on one occasion, Jesus reminded them that this could happen only by prayer[7] (Mark 9:29). The disciples had been given supernatural abilities by God to exorcise demons, but these abilities were to be employed in conjunction with prayer. God doesn't do for you what he tells you to do, but he does expect you to acknowledge your need of him in doing it. This principle holds true in your life—you have been made a new creation in Christ Jesus, a change that enables you to do that which you could not do before your conversion (Rom. 8:8). But you must do it in conjunction with prayerful dependence on the Spirit who dwells within to empower you. And again, remember that Jesus told us that God gives his Spirit to those who ask (Matt. 7:11; Luke 11:13).

All growth comes by God's grace, by obedience to his commands done in the wisdom and power of the Spirit. Sanctification is not an *either/or* matter. Sanctification (overcoming sin God's way and learning to live righteously) is always a *both/and* process—both a human and a divine process.

Repentance in Problem-Solving

One factor, however, is of the utmost importance. All that I have said (and will say) is hollow, meaningless, and worthless if this necessary factor is missing. The steps I have outlined thus far must usually be accompanied by repentance. There must be a genuine change of mind (the meaning of the New Testament

7. The words "and fasting" are not in the better texts.

term for *repentance*, which is *metanoia*) that leads to a change of direction (the meaning of the Old Testament word for the effects of repentance, which is *shuv*). In Isaiah 55:8, God tells us that our ways are not his ways and that our thoughts are not his thoughts. Repentance deals with both problems: in repentance, one's thoughts are brought into harmony with God's, and as a result, one's ways also come into harmony with God's.

The process I have suggested ought to lead to repentance. John's thoughts about women must change, and his ways of looking at and thinking about them must also change. A careful study of Proverbs 5 (not to mention several other passages from that Bible book) ought to lead to a radical change of thought about the matter of adultery. Mary likewise ought to have a change of mind as she contemplates the harm that Scripture says gossip does to others. If there is no repentance on your part, during which you find that your thinking comes into line with God's, don't settle for changing your ways. Any action you take without a new view of yourself, of your sin against God and others, and of God himself will be merely outward window-dressing. God won't bless it. Authentic, God-pleasing change will always be the fruit of genuine inner repentance, which begins with a change of mind. That is what John the Baptist was talking about when he told the people, the tax collectors, and the soldiers to produce fruit worthy of repentance (Luke 3:8). That is to say, the results of repentance (which he specified), if genuine, would flow out of their change of heart.

Getting Started

Now, using the principles and practices set forth so far, it's time for you to begin to deal with a problem or two on your own. In the space below, in one crisp sentence, write out the problem that you recognize needs solving. Before you do, however, be sure that you are thinking biblically. Remember, using biblical terminology will help. Since you may wish to refine this statement later on, *pencil* it in.

_____

_____

Next, using your concordance—you should have a comprehensive one, not just the skinny one found in the back of the Bible—locate two or three principal passages that relate either directly or indirectly to the problem. You may have to search among many to find those that are most appropriate. Don't settle for the first verse you locate, or deceive yourself by stretching a verse to mean what it obviously doesn't mean. Write their references on the lines below.

    1. _____

    2. _____

    3. _____

Third, using Bible dictionaries and commentaries (both, not merely one or the other), *study* these passages in their context to determine what the words say, what purpose the writer had when penning them, and how they pertain to your problem. If you don't know what a commentary is, ask your pastor. He should be able to put you on the track of a few to begin with. After studying diligently, write out your conclusions in the spaces below.

What does each chosen verse *mean*?

    1. _____

    2. _____

    3. _____

How did the writer intend to *change* readers by each one?

1. _____

2. _____

3. _____

What *specific*, concrete change does each verse indicate I should make?

1. _____

2. _____

3. _____

Having answered those three questions, answer one more:

How will making those changes solve my problem?

_____

_____

Now, when you lay out the elements necessary for utilizing these Scripture truths to solve your problem, be sure to include:

That which must be put off—thoughts, attitudes, practices, and the like that must be eliminated ("cut off the right hand," for instance, as in Matthew 5:30).

_____

_____

That which must be put on in their place—that is, the biblical alternatives (in addition to the cessation of lying, Paul says to put on truth-telling in Ephesians 4:25).

_____

_____

Write out the specific actions that you plan to take when faced with the problem:

_____

_____

_____

Further Preparation

Now that you have done all of this, let me suggest the following in addition: before facing a problem, pray regularly for wisdom and strength to solve it God's way. Don't wait until the problem has become so imminent that you are forced to take action. You do not want to act under pressure when you can avoid doing so. Here is what God says about hasty action: "Desire without knowledge is not good; and whoever makes haste with his feet misses his way" (Prov. 19:2). If you attempt to solve problems *without knowledge* of what God wants you to do, and how he expects you to do it, you'll foolishly disregard this important principle—and you will miss your way and sin. If, on the other hand, instead of acting hastily, you plan the godly ways that you intend to follow in solving your problems, and then follow through on such biblically based plans, you will act wisely and can expect God to help you.

So what is the sum of what you have read so far? Simply this: God expects you to solve problems, to solve them his way, and to avail yourself of those resources (his Word, his Spirit, your new ability to please him) that he has provided as you do so. May he encourage you through the reading and implementing of these words to tackle and solve problems that have been a difficulty for so long. While you now have the fundamental process of sanctification in view, a basic plan for solving problems God's way, and some examples of how this takes place in the day-to-day course of life, we still need to consider some other matters.

A Crucial Element

Everything that you have been reading so far will mean nothing if you fail to follow through. As you attempt to solve a problem, you must be willing to commit yourself to the task. There should be no shortcuts, no glossing over of the more difficult aspects of the process as you hurry to find relief. Repentance, for example, must be thorough and proceed from a genuine desire to please God. It is easy enough to go through the motions without meaning it, only to complain when nothing changes. I am speaking about *commitment*.

Commitment is your determination to put forth a wholehearted effort that, regardless of the difficulties encountered, will not allow you to become discouraged and quit, but rather will encourage you to continue until there is success. There may be times when the outcome looks bleak, times when hard or unpleasant tasks are required. But if you're committed, these won't deter you. And there is even more—commitment usually involves at least five factors:

1. *Knowing what you're getting into.* If you don't understand— at least generally—what will be required, it'll be difficult (if not impossible) to commit yourself to the process. Commitment to an unknown ordinarily can't be true commitment. It'll fall apart under stress, times when you recognize that what you thought you might be doing turns out to be quite different, and other such circumstances.

2. Having a desire to do whatever is required. While you shouldn't attempt to commit yourself to an unknown, in like manner it's all but impossible to commit yourself when you learn what is required of you but are not concerned about accomplishing it. A subtle twist here must be recognized. When the elements involved in pursuing a task are unpleasant and undesirable in and of themselves, you may still genuinely commit yourself to that task out of a desire to please God. It is therefore possible to commit yourself to do even very difficult or undesirable tasks. Paul, thousands of martyrs, and others have gone through torture and even death out of a desire to please their Lord. So it is vital that you understand what you are committing yourself to— fundamentally, the commitment to honor God by completing a given task, desirable or not.

3. Having what it takes to pull it off. You may know what it is you're getting into, and you may desire to do it in order to please God. But if you don't have the resources required to achieve it, the so-called commitment is in vain. It is foolish, for instance, for one who doesn't know how to speak to commit himself to a speaking engagement. It is meaningless for another to commit himself to building an addition to his house when he doesn't have the funds to do so, or the tools, or the required skills. He may desire to do so, but it won't happen. It is no commitment when you commit yourself to an impossibility.

4. Laying out a plan for doing what needs to be done. In this regard, you have already been given a basic plan for solving problems that you may use, modify, or replace. But whatever you do, you must know the outcome you desire, the steps involved in reaching it, and what skills and other resources are necessary to get the job done. In other words, you must sketch out what you'll do, in what order you'll do it, and what is necessary for you to do it. You may even find it wise to schedule when various parts of the plan should be completed.

27

5. Doing what has been planned. Too often, great plans have failed precisely because they were altered, misunderstood, or simply not followed. Unless you actually begin the project and then persevere, the best-laid plans will mean nothing.

If you neither understand nor become committed to whatever the Lord expects you to do in order to solve a problem, you will fail. Therefore, it is vital not only to know what commitment requires, but also to *become* committed, in the full sense of what that means.

Solving Problems with Others

Another factor that you must consider is the involvement of other people. Many solutions will require the consent, backing, or help of others. If, for example, the solution to a problem involves gaining permission to do it, raising enough money to accomplish it, or enlisting the right people to assist with it, you'll have to learn how to work with people. Not only must you be able to gain agreement, but as the solution is in the process of being worked out, you must learn to maintain proper relations as well. In other words, because some solutions need an ability to work well with others, they will be stalled if you fail to relate appropriately to those people. This is no place to spell out all that is necessary to ensure successful working relations, but perhaps it is enough to point out that if you're already doing what God requires of you, you ought to be able to work well with others.

One of the problems in working with others in order to reach a solution to a problem is the desire that others may have to set forth their own plans for solving the problem you are jointly tackling. They may suggest unbiblical changes to your plans, want to take shortcuts, be unwilling to follow directions, and so forth. Successfully handling such short-term problems that must be solved in order to solve the greater one can be vital.

Insist on your plan if it is the best one. If others have ideas that are inconsistent with yours, be firm. Thank them for their interest, their suggestions, and the like, but explain that you have devoted much thought and prayer to the task and are convinced that your way is the one that you must follow. At times, this may mean losing support or assistance from others, but if that is necessary, so be it. You don't want to lose such people, and you may have to explain in detail at some length why you believe you should proceed according to your plan. But if, even after taking time, those with whom you are working still disagree, you may have to ask whether they are willing to go on with the effort you are making as planned. If not, it may be necessary to release them from any obligations they have assumed and to search for help from others.

Of course, some solutions involving other people may require the assistance or agreement of those who cannot be replaced. They are the only ones who can be involved. Such relationships may be tricky, but must be handled properly. Behind everything, naturally, you will be asking God to bless and bring agreement to everyone involved. Don't give in if it is absolutely necessary to follow your plan in order to solve the problem, but if the task has a nonessential aspect that you may agree to alter in favor of a suggestion from another, then by all means, make the alteration! In that way, the one making the suggestion will consider himself a vital part of the endeavor.

The Time Factor

Still another matter to think about is time. How much time are you willing to spend to be sure that you are solving the problem well—that is, biblically? As I have indicated, it does take time to know your Bible well enough to bring it properly into the problem-solving process. Because of this, you may find that you must free up time for doing so. Someone says, "I don't think that I have any time to free up." This might be so in your case, too. But even if there isn't time to do what needs to be done to please God, you must find the time to do it. Most people waste far more time than they realize. Some nickel-and-dime it away—in little bits and pieces lost here and there. These pieces, cobbled together, might constitute quite a block of time. Think about how you might reclaim those otherwise lost hours. Study, which I have suggested that you need to do in order to understand and appropriate the truths of the Bible, cannot be done in short periods of time. It requires blocks. If you are one of those who have problems finding time to study, you need to discover what frivolously spent hours ought to be replaced by worthwhile activity.

"You don't know my situation." Of course I don't. But I do know that if you are a true believer, and you don't know your Bible from personal study, as well as from what you learn at church, then something is wrong. And reclaiming time is probably at least one item on the hit list that you should think about. How about it, Christian?

When Your Solution Is Wrong

You will make wrong decisions about how to solve problems because you are not yet perfect. You make mistakes that grow out of the lack of knowledge, as the result of prejudice, stubbornness, unbiblical attitudes, pressure, and any number of other causes. What must be done when this happens?

First, you must admit the fact to yourself and to anyone else who may need to know. Certainly you should talk to God about it. The bad solution may well require repentance. Repentance, as we have seen, involves not only the confession of one's failures (and of sin, if that is the case), but also the taking of action. This action should grow out of and be fitting to your change of mind. It may involve righting wrongs that could include monetary payment or other such concrete steps that you should take. When restitution for wrong solutions has been made, then you must next go about correcting other effects of a wrong solution, if that is possible. Doing so may involve the help of a truly biblical counselor when you are perplexed about what to do. I say "truly" because not all who describe themselves as such really are biblically oriented. To turn to them would be another wrong solution.

Conclusion

If you've learned something from reading this booklet that you did not know before, good. But if you don't put what you have learned to work, bad. You have wasted your time. Think about the way in which you formerly solved problems, and when you must do so on the next occasion, apply the biblical problem-solving principles that you've learned here instead.